10|21

D0187086

At the Crossroads of the Scriptures

At the Crossroads of the Scriptures

An Introduction to Lectio Divina

Ghislaine Salvail

With a Foreword
by Father Marc-Daniel Kirby, O.Cist.

Translated by
Paul C. Duggan

BOOKS & MEDIA
BOSTON

Library of Congress Cataloging-in-Publication Data

Salvail, Ghislaine.
  [Au carrefour des Ecritures. English]
  At the crossroads of Scripture : an introduction to Lectio
Divina / Ghislaine Salvail.
    p. cm.
  Includes bibliographical references.
  ISBN 0-8198-0765-6
  1. Prayer—Catholic Church. 2. Spiritual life—Catholic
Church. 3. Bible—Devotional use. I. Title.
BX2350.65.S25   1996
248.3—dc20   96-24538
                                            CIP

Original title: *Au Carrefour des Écritures*
Copyright © 1994, Éditions Paulines, 3965, boul. Henri-Bourassa Est, Montréal, QC, Canada, and Médiaspaul 8, rue Madame, 75006, Paris, France.

Cover art: M. Christopher Meagher, FSP

http://www.pauline.org
E-mail: PBM_EDIT@INTERRAMP.COM

Printed and published in the U.S.A. by Pauline Books & Media, 50 St. Paul's Avenue, Boston, MA 02130.

Pauline Books & Media is the publishing house of the Daughters of St. Paul, an international congregation of women religious serving the Church with the communications media.

1 2 3 4   99 98 97 96

Table of Contents

Acknowledgment

$\mathcal{B}$efore they begin to read this book, I wish to inform the readers that this path of prayer would never have seen the light of day without the inestimable help of Father Marc-Daniel Kirby, O. Cist.

His precise notes made my research easier. His clear teaching allowed me to integrate the method easily. Finally, his communicative enthusiasm aroused in me the desire to share my prayer experience.

He has left his mark both in my spiritual life and in this modest work which I offer for your reading. May the Word of God be glorified by it!

G. S.

Open my eyes, so that I might see
marvelous things in your law.
Lord, lift the veil over my heart
whenever I am reading the Scriptures.
May you be blessed, Lord:
teach me your wishes.
Word of the Father, give me your word
and touch my heart:
enlighten the senses of my heart.
Open my lips, and fill them with your praise.
Be in my heart, Lord, and in my mouth.
Be in my mouth, so that with honesty and dignity
I might proclaim your oracles,
with the power of the most Holy Spirit sanctifying me.
O you, the two-natured coal who,
touching the prophet's lips, purified him of his sin,
Touch my lips as well, I who am a sinner;
make me free from all stain
and able to proclaim your oracles.
Lord, open my lips, and my mouth will tell your praise.

Lancelot Andrewes (1555-1626),
Livre d'Heures, Paris DDB

Foreword

*L*ike a flame passed from candle to candle, the practice of *lectio divina* is being passed from the desert to the city, from the silence of the cloister to the heart of countless Christians in the world. To an ever increasing number of men and women the daily practice of *lectio divina* is a source of fire and light. "Were not our hearts burning within us while he was talking to us on the road, while he was opening the Scriptures to us?" (Lk 24:32). This book is the fruit of one woman's desire to transmit the flame she herself received in the quiet of a Cistercian abbey.

Lectio divina is not a specifically monastic approach to prayer. It is a remarkably simple way of prayer, within the reach of all who hunger and thirst for the experience of God. *Lectio divina* is closer to listening to God than to reading about him, closer to seeing him "in a mirror dimly" (1 Cor 13:12) than to studying a text, closer to "tasting that the Lord is good" (cf. Ps 34:8) than to acquiring a purely intellectual knowledge of him.

Lectio divina begins with the desire for God. Even more profoundly, it begins with the awareness of God's desire for us. The Word of God is the place in which these two desires meet: God's yearning to communicate himself, his adorable mystery, his unutterable love; and the yearning of every human heart to receive the "Gift of God" (Jn 4:10), to see his glory (cf. Ex 33:18), to receive the very kiss of his love (cf. Song 1:2). Desire, or at least the desire of desire, is the one prerequisite for *lectio divina.*

Lectio divina cannot be separated from the full liturgical life of the Church. The Word of God attains its fullest and richest resonances when it is proclaimed, sung and heard in the Church's liturgy. The Liturgy of the Hours and of the Eucharist, celebrated according to the yearly, weekly and daily rhythms of the Church's calendar, is the source of *lectio divina* and its summit. The asceticism of *lectio divina* includes a personal "obedience" to the liturgical lectionary. *Lectio divina* is most fruitful when it draws upon the liturgy and returns to it.

Lectio divina is not an occasional practice of devotion. It is a way of life. It requires patience, generosity, steadfastness, perseverance and the willingness to make a daily sacrifice of time. *Lectio divina* does not bear fruit overnight. Weeks and months, and more often than not years, may go by before one begins to perceive signs of an inner transformation. Almost imperceptibly the Word of God takes root deep in the heart, sprouts, grows and bears fruit for the glory of the Father and the joy of the Church.

Sister Ghislaine's book seeks only to pass on the flame. In closing it, the reader will want to open the book of the Scriptures and descend into the depths of the heart by means of the four-runged ladder: *lectio, meditatio, oratio* and *contemplatio.* Once the eyes of faith have become adjusted to the dark brightness wherein the Word reveals himself, there will be a moment of recognition. The face of Christ will begin to emerge from the sacred page, shining through the text as through a lattice (cf. Song 2:9). The Scriptures will become a pure water for the irrigation of the heart, a living water capable of quenching every thirst, a daily bread, a medicine and a balm.

Father Marc-Daniel, O.Cist.
Monk of the Cistercian Abbey
of Our Lady of Nazareth
Rougemont, Quebec

Saint Anselm's Abbey
Washington, D.C.
April 25, 1995

Preface

"He is going ahead of you to Galilee" (Mt 28:7)

*W*hen the Lord calls us to the desert, it is in order to lead us back to Galilee, where the cries and appeals of our contemporaries await us. Yet what is this "Galilee of the nations" (or of the pagans) that Matthew is talking about?

First, we should know that, historically, this region situated in northern Palestine was invaded several times by the Assyrians and the Chaldeans, which led to a mixed population and the presence of many pagans. Consequently, the people of Galilee developed a curious accent that other Jews easily recognized and scorned them for. We can recall what some bystanders said to Peter during Jesus' passion: "After a little while the bystanders came up and said to Peter, 'Certainly you are also one of them, for your accent betrays you'" (Mt 26:73).

For all these reasons, Galilee did not have a good reputation. Yet it was from there that Jesus was sending his disciples "to the lost sheep of the house of Israel" (Mt 10:6). And it was largely in this region that he fulfilled his earthly mission.

Jesus said to them, "Go!" It was a command to mission.... The message directed to the disciples and to Peter is twofold:

first, to announce the resurrection, and then to summon them to Galilee (cf. Mk 16:7). Christ was going before them. He is always the Master who goes ahead and who is to be followed.

The true disciple is the one who sets out to follow the Master by trusting in him. This is why the same verbs reoccur at each calling: "Come, follow me" (Jn 1:43; Mt 8:19-22; 16:24; Lk 5:11, 27; 9:49; 18:22).

Mark further adds, "There you will see him, just as he told you" (Mk 16:7). From that time, Jesus continues to be seen by his disciples. True, he is no longer part of the world perceived by the senses, but rather of the world of God. Thus, he cannot be seen except by those whom he allows to see himself. To see him in this way involves one's heart, spirit and inner openness.

In the evangelical accounts of the appearances of the risen Lord, Jesus shows himself to people's senses; nevertheless, he can only address the senses which look beyond the sensory (cf. Jn 20:11-17).

This allowed us to write, in a poem entitled *Before the Empty Tomb:*

> You, Mary Magdalene,
> you see the stone removed
> and you weep over his stolen body.
> You weep over yourself,
> And so you cannot recognize him
> In the gardener....
> He had to call your name
> So that you might open your eyes
> And that the Rabbouni might step forth.

The experience of *lectio divina* is an experience of attentive listening to the Lord who speaks to us in our hearts.

Guigo the Carthusian asserted that the more we know the revealed Word of God, not just in a superficial way but with an in-depth experiential knowledge, the better we can see him in our brothers and sisters and witness to him in the heart of our modern Galilee.

We should also be aware of our accent, if I may so express myself at the risk of being misunderstood. Think of the meeting-place to which we are summoned: Jesus goes before us; therefore he is waiting for us. Let us go join him in all trust.

We cherish just one hope: that this book might lead you to try the experience of the daily *lectio divina*. If you already practice and are faithful to this spiritual experience, then may this reading serve to make you more receptive to the Word. May it sharpen your hunger and your thirst for this Word which, nonetheless, always leaves us hungry and never quenches our thirst, since the Word sustains an insatiable desire here below. Teresa of Avila understood it well when she wrote, "Our desire is never satisfied."

The Word of God constitutes a message from God to the human person. It is a call from God addressed to the person so that she might know God from within her being, that she might encounter Christ and that she might live for him and no longer for herself.

> In the spiritual life, the Word of God cannot be presented as an ideological statement. Nor can it be reduced to a book from which theology and catechesis draw inspiration.

> Thus, the Word of God should be read in faith. It should be penetrated and understood under the action of the Spirit, as a Word coming from God and leading to God.

> Biblical studies have made great progress. The Bible has become widely distributed in recent times, especially since Vatican Council II. We should rejoice in this. Yet, despite this fine effort, I believe the results are somewhat deceptive. Too often we approach the Bible

in too intellectual a manner without sufficient openness to wisdom.

The intellect speculates, seeks to meditate and to know
ever more. On the contrary, wisdom comes to know
(in the biblical sense, the heart is the seat of knowledge), to pray, to taste *(sapiens* = sapere, to taste).

This is not necessarily a matter of grasping the meaning
of the Word which is read by relying on scriptural
proofs, nor of gathering the fruits proceeding from
scholarly exegetical research. No, it is a matter of being
attentive to spiritual intuitions apt to nourish us at the
moment of the reading.[1]

The aim of *lectio divina* (divine reading) consists in
grasping the spiritual meaning of the Word and in discovering
the fruits that it is offering at every moment.

As an example, we can quote Bernard of Clairvaux who,
better than anyone else, was able to give a mystical meaning to
the Word.

Let us listen to him giving his spiritual commentary on
Genesis 2:10, where it states that, in Paradise, four rivers issue
from a single source:

Four springs flow out of the depth of the heart of Christ,
and these four streams of water irrigate the Church
throughout the whole world.

These four springs are truth, wisdom, power and love.
It is from these four springs that we draw water, different water from each one *(Div* 96, 1).

Bernard was convinced that the Word possesses a won-
drous unity, that it always has something useful to give to us,
and that it is always open to several meanings.

These intuitions are given to us at the precise moment
that the reading penetrates our hearts. Once again, they cannot

be identified with the conclusions of some other research which is pursuing other aims for another purpose. It is important to differentiate between these two levels.

I will conclude this long introduction by quoting Francois Varone, that man of stunning clarity, regarding the spiritual thirst and striving of his contemporaries. Varone states that "Only the word of God, at first listened to, and then finding the human experience in which it can dwell and manifest itself, can provide a reference for turning into faith."[2]

1

The Word as a Seed

The Word of God can be compared to a seed that sprouts by itself (cf. Mk 4:26-29). It contains life in itself: "This is no trifling matter for you, but rather your very life," Moses told the Israelites (Deut 32:47). The Word of God springs up in history, as in the field of the personal life of every man and woman, as the great tree of the kingdom (cf. Mt 13:31).

In the explanation of the parable of the sower in Mark 4:13-20, Jesus says, "The sower sows the word," and at the end he adds: "And these are the ones sown on the good soil: they hear the word and accept it and bear fruit, thirty and sixty and a hundredfold" (Mk 4:20).

In order for the Word to produce fruit, acceptance is undoubtedly required, yet it must always be remembered that it is God who gives growth. "I planted," Paul would say, "Apollos watered, but God gave the growth" (1 Cor 3:6-7).

What a comfort it is for our absolute powerlessness to be invited to trust and hope: "Apart from me you can do nothing" (Jn 15:5).

We must remember that the Word is an unpredictable seed. Who would have suspected that the seed of God, fallen into the womb of an unknown girl hidden in the midst of a small Galilean village, would give a Savior to the world?

17

Who could predict the path we took after our baptism, when the first seed was sown? Every day a seed, a Word, is given to us to eat; a Word is held...who can predict its fruit?

The Word can change hearts. Gregory the Great, the Latin Father of the Church born in Rome around 540, was convinced of this. He wrote:

> A person sows the seed in the soil when he plants a good intention (a good desire) in his heart. After doing so, he must, in relying on hope, lean on God. He lies down at night and gets up in the morning, because he keeps on going in the midst of successes and failures. The seed sprouts and grows without his knowing it, because even though he might not harvest the fruit of this progress, once virtue is put in motion it advances toward its own realization. The soil brings forth fruit by itself because, predisposed by grace, the human soul, by itself, advances toward the fruit of good works. Yet this same soil at first produces the stalk, then the ear, and then the full fruit within the ear. To produce the stalk is still to feel that good will is weak. To reach the ear is when virtue develops and drives us to multiply good works. The ripe wheat is when virtue has made such progress that the person has attained fullness of action and of constancy in the accomplishment of duty. When the wheat is ripe, the scythe is put to use, since it is all God's crop, a harvest belonging to him.

Jacques Belanger, O.F.M. Cap., told this true story during a conference that he gave to a group of religious sisters:

> Some Capuchin Fathers had set up a perfume factory on Nosy Be, an island of Madagascar. After sixty years of operation, this factory passed into the hands of two Swiss brothers (laymen). They would work there all day long. In the evening, after bathing and changing their clothes, they went for refreshment to the terrace bar of

Tananarive, the nearest city, which was still a good distance from their factory.

People already seated would say, "The perfumers must be coming soon; we can smell their perfume." Or again: "The perfumers have arrived; a fragrance is floating in the air."

Try as they might, the scent clung to their skin!

Since we are disciples of Jesus and we draw upon his Word every day, our contemporaries should, upon approaching us, not only recognize our accent but should also smell the fragrance of Jesus Christ on the paths of the kingdom where we walk. This perfume should go before us. Then we can make our own the words of the Song of Solomon (1:3): "Your anointing oils are fragrant; your name is perfume poured out; therefore the maidens love you."

Prayer

Unforeseeable seed!
One day, in a little village of Galilee
in the womb of the amazed Virgin Mary,
you sowed the seed of your kingdom,
the creator Love:
Jesus Christ, your Word,
your beloved Son.
Unforeseeable seed!
Every day, in the depths of our humanity,
you sow the seed of your life,
the Word of Jesus, your Firstborn.
In the womb of the astonished Mary,
in my heart of free man and woman,
in the depths of our humanity, I know not how,
Jesus has bloomed, your Word has grown
and Mary, my heart and the earth

have given him their fruit.
Unforeseeable seed!
One day, the day of my baptism,
in my heart of free man and woman,
you sowed the seed of your kingdom:
saving Love: the life of the risen Jesus.[3]

2

We Are a Chosen Race

Peter said to the Christians of his time: "But you are a chosen race, a royal priesthood, a holy nation, God's own people, in order that you may proclaim the mighty acts of him who called you out of darkness into his marvelous light" (1 Pet 2:9).

Peter is applying to Christians what was said of the people of the old covenant: "I give water in the wilderness...to give drink to my chosen people" (Isa 43:20). "You shall be for me a priestly kingdom and a holy nation" (Ex 19:6).

The liturgy of the Mass of Chrism uses the same language at the blessing of the oils and the consecration of the chrism: "By the mystery of this holy chrism, you bestow upon us the riches of your grace. Indeed, your children, after being reborn in the water of baptism, are strengthened by the anointing of the Spirit and, made in the likeness of Christ, they share in his prophetic, priestly and royal function."

But what do these words mean for us today? Let us point out right away that we affirm with Peter that every believer is priest, prophet, king and saint, and that these four characteristics are essential for anyone undertaking *lectio divina*. That said, what is the best way to make us understand this truth as the baptized Christians that we are?

We must admit that, of all these teachings, this was the most difficult to elaborate. A poor concept of our Christian originality, maintained for a long time, has warped people's outlook. That is why people find it hard to convince themselves that these four spiritual types form part of our heritage, of our rich patrimony.

Enzo Bianchi, whose book *Prier la parole* was the origin of this work, expressly states that every believer is a priest, prophet and king, and that these are the essential and indispensable qualities for having the power and the right to do *lectio divina*.[4]

A priest actualizes an historical event in the present day. He makes Christ present in our world; he commemorates his coming. Through the priest, the Word becomes the sign or sacrament of this presence. This is what allowed Maurice Zundel to assert that "Scripture is a true sacrament behind which we must look for the face of Love."[5] He then states that it is fair to say that, as lovers of the Word, we are priests.

In my opinion, this term has been reserved in the Catholic tradition for too long to ordained ministers. However, for Peter as for the authors of the Letter to the Hebrews and of the Book of Revelation and of the whole New Testament, the baptized share in the unique priesthood of Jesus Christ: "through the power of an indestructible life...you are a priest forever" (Heb 7:16, 17). He "made us to be a kingdom, priests serving his God and Father" (Rev 1:6; 5:10), "since those rescued by Christ are kings and priests with him."[6]

Jesus accomplished his mission of making the Father known. He is continuing this mission now through the new people that we are, people born of his death and resurrection. This is why Christians receive this particular priesthood which enables them to offer the true sacrifice which is nothing else than their own lives, persons and actions, offered to God in thanksgiving.

True, in the midst of this priestly people, some receive a particular ministry for the service of their brothers and sisters. Moreover, Peter has something to say about this at the end of his letter: "I exhort the elders [presbyters = heads of the community] among you to tend the flock of God that is in your charge..." (1 Pet 5:1-2).

This does not serve to exclude ordinary Christians from the priestly people. We can say that the table upon which the book of the Word is resting becomes, for the one familiar with the Word, the altar on which God comes down.

The King, the Lord, realizes the Word in salvation history, in the sense that he consecrates history in order to make it into a saving history. Israel's king was looked on as a savior. He was the protector of the widow and the orphan. He was anointed by the Lord, and the one receiving the anointing belongs from then on to the people of God, which is also called to realize the Word within history.

We were anointed at baptism and confirmation. We were consecrated by the unction. "Be sealed with the Holy Spirit, the gift of God" *(Ritual of Confirmation)*. We are then witnesses of salvation history and we too must realize this salvation in the heart of our Galilee. This is what is called "making the kingdom of God come." This kingdom of God is not so much a place as it is a special relationship between God and his creature, most especially with the poor: "For the Lord, the Most High, is awesome, a great king over all the earth. He subdued peoples under us, and nations under our feet" (Ps 47:3-4).

In this sense, ever since the coming of Jesus, we are participants in the kingship of God, because he is at the side of the weak and of anyone trusting in him. We cannot say it enough: the kingdom is at work like a seed placed by God in the heart of every human being.

In the Old Testament, the prophet was a person called by God to fulfill a special mission in which his will was subordinated to that of God, which was communicated to him by direct inspiration. Thus, the prophet was a charismatic guide, directly sent by Yahweh to alert his people to the dangers and attractions of evil in all its forms, and to preach reform and the renewal of an authentic morality.

Thus we can say that the classical prophets, for the most part, had the experience of an entirely unique intervention by God at one time or another in their lives. One does not just simply decide to become a prophet. The people do not delegate someone, even if hand-picked, to be a prophet. God alone chooses a prophet for himself, with complete freedom and gratuitousness.

It is easy to prove this assertion. We have only to compare the category of prophets with that of priests in Israel. These latter were, to use a common phrase, very "contingent." The priesthood for example, was reserved only to the men of the tribe of Levi and to the descendants of Aaron. Therefore, the Old Testament priesthood was hereditary. Moreover, it was necessary to meet some special criteria if one wished to be judged suitable for exercising the priestly function: the priest could not be tonsured nor shaven on the sides of the face, and must have abstained from approaching the dead (cf. Lev 21:5-11).

To become a prophet, no restriction of this kind was required. Among the tribes of Israel, no one could arrogate to himself the right of prophetic offspring. These chosen ones came from different social spheres. Thus, Jeremiah was the son of a priestly family. One's state of life had no bearing upon being declared a prophet.

We know well the story of Hosea, whose marriage played the role of an unpredecented symbolic action. In contrast, Jeremiah's celibacy was quite significant in his prophetic mission: "The Word of the Lord came to me: 'You shall not take a wife, nor shall you have sons and daughters in this place'" (Jer 16:1).

In a word, the calling can come in different ways and the

mission can vary endlessly. The nature of a prophet is evident in this. His destiny will mark him out this way.

In the New Testament, the prophet is the one who makes the Word heard. This is what Peter meant when he said to the elect living abroad in the dispersion (the *diaspora* referred to the Jews living outside of Palestine; today it is applied to Christians scattered through the world): "But you are...God's own people, in order that you may proclaim the mighty acts of him who called you out of darkness into his marvelous light" (1 Pet 2:9).

We must add that around Jesus there were people who also prophesied: Zechariah, Anna, and above all John the Baptist. Jesus also appeared as a prophet (cf. Mt 16:4), but he did not claim the title. He contented himself with acting as a prophet by denouncing the excesses of the religious leaders and the Jews (cf. Mt 15:7).

He revealed the content of the signs of the times (cf. Lk 12:54-56). He acknowledged that he was consecrated to the tragic lot typical of the prophets (cf. Mt 23:37).

Obviously, Jesus takes his place above the prophets, since he himself achieves our salvation (cf. Lk 10:24) and speaks his words on his own authority (cf. Mt 7:28-29). Yet it is from him that we should draw the example of being a prophet today through being familiar and intimate with the Word, as well as through denouncing anything not in conformity with Gospel values.

The Word challenges us; by the power of the Holy Spirit, it can change hearts. Thus it becomes efficacious: "The word of God is living and active" (Heb 4:12). The prophet is a witness. He must bring into deeds the Word that he has read, meditated, prayed, contemplated....

In the Bible holiness is proper to God. Yet it can also characterize a person or a thing. It signifies that a new relation is established between God and that person.

In the New Testament, the "newness" consists in the fact that the saint is someone who accepts the gift of God, the new life in Jesus. The call to holiness can only be understood in Jesus, God's Holy One.

We recall that Paul was the first to call Jesus' disciples saints, not because of their moral perfection but because of a vocation through which God calls them as members of his consecrated people and entrusts them with a mission: "To all God's beloved in Rome, who are called to be saints: Grace to you and peace from God our Father and the Lord Jesus Christ" (Rom 1:7). It goes without saying that this vocation implies and requires holiness of life.

Being committed to following the same path as Jesus, the disciple accepts being abased and humbled. Yet, according to the theology of Peter, he does so while seeking to become more and more like Christ and not to gain his own glory. Thus, this admonition addressed to women of his time can also benefit all the baptized:

"Do not adorn yourselves outwardly...rather, let your adornment be the inner self with the lasting beauty of a gentle and quiet spirit" (1 Pet 3:3-4).

The saints are those who always follow Peter's counsels addressed to Jesus' disciples, namely to those who were living in the *diaspora:* "In your hearts sanctify Christ as Lord. Always be ready to make your defense to anyone who demands from you an accounting for the hope that is in you" (1 Pet 3:15).

According to Vatican II, Christian holiness consists in union with Christ: "In the Church, all those who belong to the hierarchy or are governed by it are called to holiness according to the Apostle's word: 'For this is the will of God, your sanctification' (1 Th 4:3)" *(Lumen Gentium,* n. 39).

This holiness should develop according to each person's vocation: "In the various classes and differing duties of life, one and the same holiness is cultivated by all, who are moved by the Spirit of God.... Each person must walk unhesitatingly according to his personal gifts and duties in the path of living faith, which arouses hope and works through charity *(Lumen Gentium,* n. 41).

Finally, a saint is always a family member in the Word, since this daily contact makes him closer to his brothers and sisters, more attentive to their needs, more respectful, more understanding.

Therefore, our personal holiness contributes to advancing the kingdom. I should be able to say: since I, a Christian, a friend and disciple of Jesus, have passed this way over this earth, this earth has become better, and "because of the progress in my life," as St. Bernard said, my brothers and sisters are enriched by my contact or, at least, they have not gone backward!

Prayer

"There is only one sadness, that we are not saints" (Leon Bloy).

> What else is being holy, Lord, than to do your will?
> And your will is written from day to day
> Every morning on the blank page of my life.
> I know, Lord,
> That it is the life of the saints that renews the Church.
> Give me a share in this renewal in my own humble way....
> Lord, in order to become a saint,
> I need only light and truth.
> Grant them to me
> and with them will come holiness....
> Recall your promise:
> "You shall be for me a holy nation" (Ex 19:6).
> And make us work together
> for its realization. Amen!

3

The Roots of Lectio Divina

*F*or those who are new at it, it is good to ask what *lectio divina* consists of as a path of contemplation or as a mystical experience. Yes, I said mystical. For too long this word has been reserved to define this experience as being a charism reserved to people out of the ordinary. Why? Simply because there was, especially in the nineteenth century, an abundance of revelations which attracted curiosity and which led people to believe that the mystical life and mysterious phenomena are the same.

Moreover, even today, visions and private revelations are numerous, and they are always called mystical. From this comes the notion that mystical experience is meant for others rather than for us, a leap of thought that is all too quick.

Having said this, this path does not therefore cease to be an experience of interiority and immediacy which helps us approach the Totally Other in a privileged manner. It is a matter of a search for unity, communion and presence. It is realized in the course of *lectio divina*. This is what made Augustine say that "*lectio divina* consists simply in seeking Christ and seeking him again." According to Origen, it signifies "consuming mysteriously the broken Word." Or again, according to Gregory of Nazianzen, it is a matter of "consuming the paschal Lamb."

Lectio divina is indeed a sacred and divine reading, yet more than a reading. This last term is too general and impoverishes it. It is not a study, a term which is too intellectual. In contrast, *lectio divina* is different from meditation which at times can become simply an effort of the will.

It is necessary to keep the Latin term *lectio divina,* or else to translate it, if one insists, by "prayed Word," or by the expression "to pray the Word." To understand this kind of prayer, it is necessary to place *lectio divina* in its historical context. Let us note at the start that it is a patrimony of the Church. It was practiced early on by the Fathers of the Church and by monks.

Yet despite the efforts of a Jerome who preached by example, or of a Bernard who said, "I know that the Word has visited me, because of the progress in my life," *lectio divina* withdrew for long centuries from monasteries to make room for the study of the Word, and became, in time, a spiritual reading. Scripture was no longer the basic book, the book recommended as the priority. In the seventeenth century, some religious ex-changed Scripture for books dealing with the Scrip-tures. This had the effect of removing *lectio divina* from its true scriptural and doctrinal sources, forging a gap which is difficult to fill even today. However, the synagogal usage aimed at having the Torah tasted in community in a festal climate of praise, of adoration or of supplication, created by the liturgy.[7]

This manner of speaking about the Word as food was dear to the Fathers of the desert. They would write truly savory aphorisms, Father J. R. Bouchet, in his little book *Si tu cher-ches Dieu,* has compiled some of patristic making: "Eat the Gospel: learn from God who God is.... From then on, the Gospel will have for you the taste of fresh bread. Sink your teeth into it. It has been baked for you."[8]

This manner of speaking about the Word and of representing it under a symbolic form still endures in fervent Jewish environments. In his autobiography, André Chouraqui relates: "Our mothers would prepare for us cakes shaped like Hebrew letters. Steeped in honey, they would be a foretaste of the delights that we would know in gulping down the Torah."[9]

It is not that the rabbis swallowed the texts but, according to them, a forgotten voice inflection, a badly pronounced word or even a syllable could shake the entire liturgical edifice. They were thus scrupulous about beginning again. Otherwise they would have to render an account to Elohim, the privileged listener of the liturgies of his beloved people, of which they were the *Bar Mitzvah* (sons of order).

> This *lectio divina* of the synagogue flowed into daily life by the memorization of what one had heard. Memorization inscribed the word into deed. It brought into play the quality of a listening-post where the heart, the body and the spirit joined together. A whisper would express it.
>
> For the fervent Jew, this now still involves:
> —reading proclaimed aloud (heard reading);
> —memorization (retained reading);
> —reflection (pondered reading).
>
> Speaking, remembering and reflecting are the three necessary phases for the same activity.
>
> The Torah is not only at the center of existence for the people of God but, as we have said, the assimilation of its content through permanent study constitutes the noblest task for every Israelite. Ever since the first century, the rabbinical tradition has left us pearls concerning *lectio divina*:
>
> "Make the Torah your permanent occupation."
> "Where there is much knowledge of the Torah, there is much life."

"Whoever drinks in the words of the Torah has acquired life in the world to come."[10]

Finally, this practice helps us grow closer to God little by little. These words of Jesus are progressively realized in our lives: "Those who love me will keep my word, and my Father will love them, and we will come to them and make our home with them" (Jn 14:23).

Prayer

> Lord, I have chosen the bread of your Word
> because this bread is food for me.
> Hunger forces us to choose even more than justice!
> And I am hungry for the Lord!
> I have chosen the bread of your Word
> because this bread is the bread of life for me.
> Life forces us to choose
> even more than fear and death.
> And I want to live, Lord!
> I have chosen the bread of your Word
> because I need this bread.
> Need is an driving force even more than desire.
> And I have great need for you, Lord!
> And you would not believe, Lord,
> how much I aspire to the satisfaction
> promised for eternal Life....

4

Jesus and Lectio Divina

Lectio divina represents the form of reading which Jesus practiced in the synagogue of Capernaum, his adopted town: "And after getting into a boat he crossed the sea and came to his own town" (Mt 9:1). "They went to Capernaum; and when the sabbath came, he entered the synagogue and taught" (Mk 1:21).

What was he teaching, if not the word of the Father of which he was the living revelation? "Everyone who has heard and learned from the Father comes to me" (Jn 6:45).

This reading of the Word was something he also practiced in the synagogue of Nazareth, his home town, and in several others, as he made his way through Galilee: "He left that place and came to his hometown, and his disciples followed him. On the Sabbath he began to teach in the synagogue" (Mk 6:1-2).

Why insist so much on the synagogal cult which Jesus practiced? The synagogue was the place of religious assembly for Jews, both in the towns of Palestine and in the Jewish colonies in the outside world. There the sabbath was celebrated by the reading of the Prophets and of the Law, followed by a homily. Every adult Jew could speak a word about it, but the authorities normally entrusted this task to Jews versed in the Scriptures.

It would seem that Jesus was not yet perceived as one of these. Thus, when he took the book and found in it, as he unrolled it, the passage from Isaiah 61:1: "The Spirit of the Lord is upon me, because he has anointed me to bring good news to the poor..." (Lk 4:18-19), and gave it a new explanation: "Today this Scripture has been fulfilled in your hearing..." (Lk 4:21), the people were astonished. They perceived that this Word of Isaiah, several centuries old, was finding its fulfillment in Jesus' proclamation: "All...were amazed at the gracious words that came from his mouth. They said, 'Is not this Joseph's son?'" (Lk 4:21-22).

His listeners became aware that what was announced in the Scriptures was being realized in Jesus, not only because Jesus was incarnating in the present day this same Word of God, but because they saw that the prophecy was becoming reality in one of the members of their community.

See what we ourselves should continue: to give a new "today" to the Word each time that we do *lectio divina*. Without this, we are going to put ourselves on a speculative level, if not an archeological one.

"Today there has been fulfilled...." If we are also able to understand this ancient Word, we will make it current and contemporary, and we will then understand its significance in all its fullness.

In the "Today there has been fulfilled," there is the beginning of a new reality for all believers, for all the priests, kings, prophets and saints that we are. And it is in Jesus that these believers find themselves able to give to the text a new savor which will come to nourish them.

In Christ, in the events and texts of the Old and New Testament, a treasury of words is given to us, words which bring the Spirit to new life for me today. It is not without reason that Paul recommends to Timothy that he should do, not his spiritual reading, but the public reading of the sacred text:

"Until I arrive, give attention to the public reading of Scripture" (1 Tim 4:13). Paul thus gives to *lectio divina* its original sense which consists of presenting the Word as a lesson of God to his people.

Prayer

> Lord, I have been told that you spoke a long time ago.
> I have also been told that the words then had another
>   meaning
> And that in the time of nuclear power and of space ships
> We cannot understand your words
> And even less your parables.
> Who, in our rich countries,
> still sows by throwing the seeds?
> Who, plowing the immense fields of wheat,
>   still harvests with a sickle?
> Who, in the midst of purebred herds, always guards the
>   sheep day and night?
> Who, harvesting the grapes from vineyards
>   as far as the eye can see,
> still tramples the grapes with his feet?
> But by grace, Lord, spare us from the error
> Of not making your Word fruitful
> In the today of our lives,
> In the today of this world.
> Spare us from this temptation of pruning your Gospel,
> Of cutting its roots, of making breaches
>   in your teaching....
> For your Word is truth
> and your Law is deliverance,
> Today and always. Amen!

5

The Practice of Lectio Divina

*I*n every liturgy of the Word, every time I read the Word, something happens. Certain gestures, postures, actions and rites accompany this reading. This makes *lectio divina* a *ceremony,* an intimate and domestic liturgy, surely, but also a very real one.

Let us note in passing that the word "liturgy" originally meant the service of the people. Then, little by little, it was used to designate the worship service or the worship of the Lord proclaimed aloud.

In the New Testament, Christ is spoken of as a liturgical celebrant and his liturgical action is set in the context of replacing the Old Testament priesthood: "We have such a high priest, one who is seated at the right hand of the throne of the Majesty in the heavens, a minister in the sanctuary and the true tent" (Heb 8:1-2). The author of the Letter to the Hebrews continues by saying: "Now if he were on earth, he would not be a priest at all" (Heb 8:4). The writer here is speaking about the old priesthood, since Christ and his offering are not placed within the earthly system of the old priesthood.

Christian liturgy is a sharing in the priesthood of Christ. It makes us liturgical celebrants insofar as we officiate at the Word. Paul calls himself a liturgical minister of Christ for the community, thanks to his role as evangelizer: "Nevertheless on some points I have written to you rather boldly by way of reminder, because of the grace given me by God to be a minister of Christ Jesus to the Gentiles in the priestly service of the Gospel of God, so that the offering of the Gentiles may be acceptable, sanctified by the Holy Spirit" (Rom 15:15-16).

In proportion to our faith, then, the text is unrolled before our eyes and Christ explains it to our hearts. He makes it present to us by the power of his Spirit. This is why *lectio divina* should be preceded by a time of prayer. It is extremely important to prepare oneself to read the Word with a free heart.

Remote preparation *

—The vigil: prepare "the altar"; mark or choose the text and read it slowly....

Preparation of the heart is very important, because God will address us personally in his Word. We must dispose ourselves to listen.

> We must also ask God for the appropriate dispositions for receiving his Word well, in a spirit of adoration and with great respect. If purity of heart is a fruit of *lectio divina*, it is also its condition, at least in desire: "Create in me a clean heart, O God!" (Ps 51:10). Purity of sight makes the Scriptures transparent; the more a heart is pure, the more the eyes of the heart are able to discern the beloved face of Christ on the sacred page.

> When we speak of purity, we are not speaking of innocence, which is another state. An infant is innocent. The virtue of purity is something acquired and preserved, often at the price of a heroic struggle. (The word "virtue" derives from the Latin word *vir,* meaning man, virility.) Purity is the act of an adult. It is above all a grace to ask for earnestly in humble and confident

prayer: "[If] our hearts condemn us...God is greater than our hearts, and he knows everything" (1 Jn 3:20).

For the Virgin Mary, immaculate, limpid, pure and humble, the Scriptures were radiantly transparent. She discerned better than the teachers of the Law the traits of the Messiah, the face of her Son and his mystery in the Law, the Prophets and the Psalms: "But Mary treasured all these words and pondered them in her heart" (Lk 2:19).

Many people ask themselves about what texts to select. They wonder what to read. It is strongly suggested to give preference to the day's liturgy: the first reading or the Gospel, or else the psalms of the Divine Office. In this choice a grace is already expressed. In a word, it is recommended that we eat what Holy Mother the Church is serving us, since she is the one who is setting the table of the Word for us.

To look for passages according to whim would be to reduce the Bible to a book in which one would look for what one wants to find. It is necessary to let the Spirit guide us through the texts of the daily liturgy. Thus, Jerome affirmed: "To open the book of the Word and to read it is to open our sails to the Holy Spirit, without knowing on what shore we will land."[11]

However, the Gospel should be the first choice. Only the continuous reading of a biblical book, such as the Letter of Paul to the Romans or the Letters of Peter or of John can dispense us from following the lectionary. For continuity helps our assimilation, reception, memorization and concentration. It counters distraction. It is also good to read the text in its context.

—Upon waking in the morning, stir up a desire for the mystical encounter by the word of a psalm or by some other word from Scripture: "My soul thirsts for God, for the living God" (Ps 42:2). "Come, Lord Jesus!" (Acts 22:20).

Many wonder what time of day they should dedicate to *lectio divina*. It is advised to do *lectio divina* every day at the same hour (at least for about thirty minutes). This is a challenge which requires some asceticism: "At set hours, it is necessary to undertake a specific reading. A reading found by chance, without continuity, far from edifying the soul, casts it into inconsistency" (William of St. Thierry).

For this reason, *lectio divina* cannot be left to stray moments or spare time. If the time is not respected, it is impossible to expect its fruits. The ancient Fathers undertook *lectio divina* with such assiduity that they memorized long texts: "Seven times a day I praise you" (Ps 119:164).

Cassian said: "See what you must aim for by every means: apply yourself with constancy and diligence to the sacred reading until an incessant meditation pervades your spirit and, as it were, the Scripture transforms you into its likeness."

One becomes what one contemplates.... Assiduity in *lectio divina* is the thermometer of our spiritual life: "What we do not know, we learn in the Bible, and what we have learned, we keep in meditation, and what we have meditated will inspire all our actions" (Isidore of Seville).

The Word is our daily nourishment and, like every meal, it does not satisfy except at privileged moments. Certain meals are far from being feasts!

Reading in faith means simply to accept the dryness of some passage, the difficulty of understanding another or the near impossibility of applying it. Yet it is necessary to remain faithful so that it cannot be said of us, "You did not recognize the time of your visitation from God" (Lk 19:44).[12]

If we remain faithful to this holy reading, we will receive unexpected graces which will give us an anticipation of the joys of heaven. Let us remember that, of all the sufferings on earth, the deepest is the beginning of heaven here below: our discovery of the sweetness of the Spirit and the pain of still being on earth. The aged Simeon experienced this suffering: "Master, now you are dismissing your servant in peace, according to your word" (Lk 2:29).

Let us remember that a dialogue of friendship and affection is made up not only of exchanges but also of eloquent silences. They speak to God of my emptiness in the face of his fullness, which is revealed to me in his Word. Such silences are salutary, because they help us to fix our gaze on God alone. This silence makes us aware of our difficulty in truly praying. It is God who opens our lips: "O Lord, open my lips, and my mouth will declare your praise" (Ps 51:15).

Where should *lectio divina* be done? In your room, the place of intimacy, the personal cloister, the sanctuary, the desert: the place of struggle, and yet, the place of quietude as well.

Above all do not be afraid of falling into isolation: "Learning the spiritual life demands the discipline of the common life, but the delightful knowledge of God demands silence, the secret of solitude, or rather a solitary heart even in the midst of a crowd" (William of St. Thierry).

How should *lectio divina* be done? Only before an open Bible while cherishing great desire for it. Make room in yourself for it. In his treatise *The Love of God* (VII, 21), St. Bernard gives this marvelous definition of the human being, the creature of God: "God has made you a creature of desire, and your desire is God himself."[13]
Another writer has said:

You are the desire of God! It should not surprise you that things here below always leave you feeling unsatisfied. That is because you are made for more, you are made for God!

You are the desire of God! It should not surprise you that human love, as beautiful as it might be, needs vigilance to last and is often fragile. That is because at the heart of every love there should be found the love of God which is fire and light and which alone can enable you to prevail.

You are the desire of God! It should not surprise you that time seems to slip by, that it goes too quickly, that it flees and escapes you on a certain day. You are made for eternity, for a duration full of life and continuity. You have been made for the joy of a desire which only God can fulfill....

You are the desire of God! Do not be surprised if time seems too long and bores you on other days, nor if you feel stifled by everyday monotony and repetition. You have been made for eternity, for an ever-new life with God, of which its beauty will be your joy and its salvation your gladness![14]

See what you are: the desire of God! This desire, this unchangeable thirst, is God's signature, God's seal, the mark of his love.... It is the injury of Jacob which was a remembrance for him: "I have seen God face to face" (Gen 32:30). It is likewise the thorn in Paul's flesh, the mystery of which has never been revealed, but only its reason: "to keep me from being too elated" (2 Cor 12:7).

This desire in you is a capacity, an opening, a call. This desire in you is your vocation to fulfill; it is the radical exigency of your being. If you do not listen to it, it is the failure of your life. If you do listen to it, it is the success of your life. You are the desire of God! This is your grandeur and your beauty!

Teresa of Avila speaks in the same way. At the beginning of the *Interior Castle* she writes: "The soul of the just is nothing else than a paradise where God says that he takes his delights."

In *lectio divina*, God fulfills the desire which he has hollowed out in the human heart.

Prayer

> Let me know myself and let me know you
> And that I desire nothing but you alone.
> Let me forget myself and let me love you
> and let me do nothing but for you alone.
> May I become smaller in my eyes
> and you greater....
> Let me attach myself to nothing but you
> and be poor for your sake.
> Cast your gaze on me so that I might love you.
> Call me so that I might see you
> and enjoy you for all eternity. Amen.

> St. Augustine

Proximate preparation

—Kneel down and enter into a climate of silence in an attitude of adoration.

After Adam and Eve yielding to Satan's temptation, after Jacob's nocturnal combat with the angel of the Lord, after the defection of the apostles and Peter's denial, we know that only prayer can give us the strength to win. Praying the Word then becomes a favor which one can demand only while kneeling.

These very first moments are extremely important. They prepare the heart to receive the seed of the Word.

Thus they should be scrupulously observed, with care to foster the environment needed for interiority.

Whatever one will experience in these early minutes will have consequences, small or large, on the following stage. A beggar at dawn, God waits for us.[15]

Whoever has had the experience of the word of love that lets the other exist will understand from within the richness of the moment.

It is important to allow the fine flower of our desire bloom within us: "To be recognized by God and to recognize him—may this union be for my existence as a man or woman what the heart is for my body."[16]

It is this space held between God who makes me exist, and I who exist as a free being beloved of God, which is the foundation of the prayer of faith.

In this preparation of the heart to receive the Word, the Spirit has an ample share. He is the one who enlightens everyone (cf. Jn 1:9). Augustine understood this well as he gave advice to someone who had asked him about it: "Say nothing without him [the Spirit], and he will say nothing without you."

Isaac the Syrian expressed the same conviction in another way: "When the Spirit establishes his dwelling in a person, that one can no longer stop praying, because the Spirit does not cease to pray through him."

Adoration is space left for God. It has immeasurable scope and influence.

6

The Stages of Lectio Divina

The *lectio* (properly speaking)

*A*ccording to Guigo the Carthusian, the *lectio* is the applied study of the Scriptures done with an attentive spirit. It leads us to the threshold of mystery. The mystery is what we have never finished discovering....

In brief, it is a way of reading the text for itself and not by relying on a commentary, however judicious it might be. For anyone preparing to enter into contact with the Scriptures, it is important to ask that the Spirit of the Lord come to take over one's whole being. For this privileged encounter will not be made possible except on the condition of developing this basic attitude which consists in pleading for the lights of the Spirit, the unique guide of this special spiritual adventure.

This prayer before the *lectio* is suggested by Guigo the Carthusian: "Lord Jesus, you who are the Son of the living God, teach me to listen to what you tell me in the holy Scriptures, and to discover your face there."

Method:

—Slowly read the chosen text in a low voice. Audible reading lets the body participate and helps memorization. Since the divine Word became, for various reasons, a Scripture, it remains no less a word that must be heard. This reading aloud makes the soul more open to spiritual impressions and intuitions.[17]

"The reading is done with one's whole being: with the body, because normally one pronounces the words with the lips; with the memory which holds them; with the intelligence which understands their meaning. The fruit of such a reading is experience."[18]

Kiss the book of the Word. The Trappist Yves Girard said in a conference: "Love worships by embracing." Dom Delatte wrote to his monks: "The Bible is God's letter to his people; it is also a love letter, which is not read by making a grammatical analysis or a logical analysis! It is read with the eyes of the heart, and even more between the lines rather than along the lines."

A sixteenth-century abbot said: "Respect for the book is shown in a concrete manner: it is not proper to leave fingermarks on the edge, nor place a lamp on an open page." This reading is already a divine presence. It is truth revealed in Jesus.

"The writings of the saints are nothing else than a chain of scriptural texts linked together by admirable prose, yet which in its simplicity and classic sobriety simply aims at enhancing these texts" (St. Cyprian).

Let us recall the passages in Scripture which speak in this sense:

"Take [the scroll] and eat; it will be bitter to your stomach, but sweet as honey in your mouth" (Rev 10:9).

"How sweet are your words to my taste" (Ps 119:103).

"Like newborn infants, long for the pure, spiritual milk" (1 Pet 2:2).

We should not fool ourselves: this reading is not easy. True, reading is easy, but there is reading and there is reading. Experience teaches us that reading, as the first movement of *lectio divina*, cannot lead us to *contemplatio* except under certain conditions:

—if it is done well;

—if it is repeated several times;

—if it opens us to reflection which enlightens and illumines us;

—if it leads to prayer which assimilates it;

—if it ends in peace and repose in God.[19]

Monasticism originating in the East insists on this first stage.

> After you collect your thoughts by words of supplication, bow to the cross and pick up the Gospel in your hands. Place it over your eyes and over your heart. Straighten up before the cross, on your feet, without sitting on the floor and, after reading each chapter, set the Gospel on the cushion and prostrate yourself before it up to ten times and make your thanks rise toward him who has made you worthy of meditating and reading "the mystery that has been hidden throughout the ages and generations" (Col 1:26), according to Paul's word. Thanks to this exterior adoration that you make before him, the interior adoration and thanksgiving, which no fleshly tongue can express rightly, will be born in your heart.[20]

This is why each reading should be conducted peaceably, without haste, without being ambitious for knowledge (critical inquiry). The *lectio* constitutes an opening, not a conquest. It consists in reading the sacred text as if the Spirit had dictated it to us, and this is no allegory:

"When the Holy Spirit inspired the sacred text, he had in mind everyone who would read it, and this text has been written for each one in particular. Therefore, it should be read as a personal letter. In this way, our reading becomes alive; it is a direct communication with the author, the Holy Spirit currently present with the reader" (Bertrand Lefort, O.C.S.O.).

Lectio divina will yield its fruits if you read it by leaving the Spirit free from the start to make it clear to you as he wills, and in leaving God free to make you see what he wants you to contemplate. It will also do so if we leave God free to make us desire, in this light, what will become prayer, calling, offering and abandonment to love.

To grasp the meaning of the text, it is necessary to reread it several times. This slow and reflective rereading will allow the Spirit to make us understand better the import and meaning of certain phrases however well-known, whether through the liturgy or through study.

This first reading might be long, since when it is done slowly, it engraves the text on the memory just like a stylus on soft wax. Thus, the *lectio* is very important in the whole process of *lectio divina*, and it would be a mistake to neglect it or to make it a rapid stage. The rest of the exercise depends on it.

> The sacred text conceals an interior meaning, and once you gain access to it, you find everything in Scripture: the spiritual reading of the Bible and of the Fathers who interpreted it engenders fervor, contributes to conversion of life and to the struggle against Satan. On the occasion of the divine reading, a grace is granted which penetrates one's whole life (Dom Jean Leclercq).

Meditatio (pondering)

Meditatio is a studious attention of the intellect proceeding from the quest for a hidden truth. It introduces us little by little to the mystery of the Word. This is a prayer before *meditatio* suggested by Guigo:

"Lord Jesus, Son of the living God, O living Word, teach me to eat and to assimilate your Gospel so that it may transform me and make my spirit become entirely conformed to what you are and to what you will."

Method:

—Be seated and begin the reading in a low voice.

—Repeat a word or a phrase that impresses you.

—Connect this passage with another (from the Old or the New Testament).

—Write down a preferred phrase and leave it in view; this will be the day's precious gem.

The second movement harmonizes with the rhythm of the *lectio*. It is a reflection on what you read aloud. It can involve some dangers, such as a sort of haste in moving to prayer, then of moving too fast to the *oratio* which, in turn, will lead to rest in God, which is proper to *contemplatio*.

Thus it is a delicate stage, one which many people have experienced, since it is tempting to look rapidly in *meditatio* for concrete applications to one's personal and apostolic life.

This impatient searching lowers the horizon of the Word and limits it to our own dimensions. It prevents us from savoring the fullness of the mystery discovered by the reading, which is the Word heard and listened to. It must be likewise remembered that any word in Scripture cannot have at all times a concrete point of application.

Thus, one should be convinced that *meditatio* is not a work of research, analysis and exegesis; rather, it can beneficially nourish a study and change the mindset of the exegete, the student or the preacher.

One should likewise be convinced that, in order to understand the Word, it is necessary to pray it, contemplate it and adore in it the one who has revealed himself there and conceals himself there. *Meditatio* is rightly the necessary way which leads us there.

Meditatio, then, centers on the text in order to discover its richness. It lingers over unknown and striking words, over new expressions. It stops over a clause, a phrase, a pericope. It can also become a dialogue with Christ.

Here is an example of a *lectio* done in this sense: we are taking the anointing at Bethany in John 12:1-11.

This passage reveals to us, in the interior of a *meditatio*, that an action can be differently understood according to the actors' way of seeing:

—a homage of love and respect by Mary, the hostess:

"Mary took a pound of costly perfume made of pure nard, anointed Jesus' feet, and wiped them with her hair" (v. 3).

—a scandal for Judas:

"Why was this perfume not sold for three hundred denarii and the money given to the poor?" (v. 5).

—anticipation of his death for Jesus:

"She bought it so that she might keep it for the day of my burial" (v. 7).

Thus certain texts and phrases, although they had been little noticed, are clarified and become new, as if read for the first time. They become more understandable and more clear.

Others appear to come to enrich the first one....

We have set for ourselves some passages from a psalm; imperceptibly, it disappears and the soul glides unawares, all entranced, to another text of Scripture. It begins to meditate on it, but it has not yet penetrated to its depth when another new text arises in the memory and pushes away the preceding one. Meanwhile, another follows; change again! The soul thus moves from psalm to psalm, leaps from the Gospel to Paul's letters, and from there jumps to the prophets (St. John Cassian).

It is almost an inebriation of the spirit.... This description seems psychologically accurate; it shows the mental mechanism of an intellect filled with the Bible, which makes "fools of God" out of us!

A true reading, according to Cassian, that Father of the Church who lived in the fourth century and who was a close friend of Pope Leo the Great, is "one that leads us to comprehension and understanding of the Scriptures, to true knowledge." In sum, it means giving ourselves the taste of Scripture more than drawing knowledge from it. *Meditatio* is the action which consists in drawing the water which will be poured out in *oratio*. It is repetition, pondering, after the manner of Paul in the Letter to the Galatians (faith and law) or of John in his Gospel (light and darkness).

One can repeat the same word without wearying, without concern over moving ahead in the text.... Thus the Word of God speaks to me or, rather, God speaks to me, and the Word tells me and asks me what even yesterday it was not telling me and asking me.

One who listens to the Word rises to the dignity of being able to respond to it. At that moment one senses the invitation to live these words, to respond to their calls. The *oratio* can then gush forth. It is good to note that these discoveries and illuminations furnished by notes in the Bible or by other sources can be kept in our prayer-book.[21]

With regard to the preferred phrase which will remain the theme of the day, let us regard it as extremely precious and as a true presence of God at the heart of our daily life. To help convince us of this, here is a text drawn from the *Herald of Divine Love* by St. Gertrude.

Gertrude, a mystic, was a Cistercian-Benedictine nun who lived in the thirteenth century. She ardently desired to acquire some relics of the cross of Jesus so as to be able to render them veneration. She received this amazing message from the Lord:

> If you want to have some relics which have the power to attract my heart powerfully toward the one possessing them, read from one end to the other the story of my passion and attentively examine the words that I said with the greatest love. Write them down and keep them as you would relics. If you repeat them frequently within yourself, be certain that you will thus obtain my grace more efficaciously than by all other relics.... You can then believe that the most precious relics that you can possess on earth are the very tender words of love from my infinitely good heart.

We conclude with a prayer which restates the need for pondering the Word in *meditatio* so that it might open our eyes to the spiritual beauties which bloom in our world and which only the Spirit can help us to discover.

Prayer

> Lord, teach us to ponder your Word,
> To listen to the groanings of the Spirit
> who dwells in our hearts.

> Help us to discover the roots of your love,
> The little sprouts of hope,
> And the fruits of justice and peace
> Which flourish in the bosom of our world
> And which announce a new springtime
> For our world. Amen!

Oratio

The *oratio* consists in a religious application of the heart to God in order to bring to him our message of love and confidence.

This is the prayer before the *oratio* suggested by Guigo:

"Lord Jesus, Son of the living God, teach my heart to speak to the Father, with whom you continually converse in the unity of the Holy Spirit. Pierce my heart with the love that unites it to the Father, and be yourself continual prayer in me."

Method:

—Let God descend upon you (provide him with a vessel).

Prayer is not an elevation of our heart to God but a descent of God to us.

—Let your prayer spring forth: "Make room in yourself, and I will become a torrent," Jesus advised St. Angela of Foligno.

—Write your prayer after the model of Jewish prayer:

1. Exclamation: "O God...."

2. Anamnesis (from the Greek: remembrance): "You who...."

3. Supplication: "Grant to me...."

4. Doxology (proclamation of the Trinity): "You who reign...."

It must be remarked that all the prefaces, the opening prayers of the canon of the Mass, and likewise all the canons, as well as all the prayers of the Old Testament, are structured as a genuine plea, as an oral exposition of deeds.

These prayers are ranked according to three movements:

The first movement reminds God who he is: "O Lord my God, you are very great" (Ps 104:1).

Then, the second movement aims at being the remembrance of what he has done for his creatures: You "who by understanding made the heavens" (Ps 136:5).

Finally, the third movement rests upon the above-mentioned plea in order to supplicate so good and so merciful a Father: "Lord, accept my supplication" (Ps 6:9).

We should point out that the Jewish manner of praying to God did not imply, at the end, recourse to the Trinity. It is, so to speak, a manner of Christianizing our prayer. Nor did the remembrance refer to the exceptional gift of the Son by the Father.[22]

This leads us to add a fourth movement to the *oratio:* the one intended to remind us that, after the coming of Jesus, things changed greatly. Since then, we have been able to implore the Spirit of God and to rely upon the presence of Christ our advocate: "We have an advocate with the Father, Jesus Christ the righteous" (1 Jn 2:1).

Christ protects us and goes so far as to protect us from ourselves. This is why every *oratio* ends in these words: "We ask you this through Jesus and through the Spirit who dwells in our hearts, for ever and ever. Amen!"

This prayer which springs forth is a simple prayer, a spontaneous prayer. It is the result, namely the fruit, of the *lectio* and the *meditatio,* more than a means for making contact with the divine.

St. Teresa of Avila said to the Carmelites of Seville, "Prayer, prayer, prayer, my sisters." She said: "Every day I understand better the fruit of meditation, and what a soul should be before God if she seeks nothing but his glory." She also added: "We can say of those beginning in prayer that they are drawing water from wells with great difficulty, as I did, since it is hard for them to recollect their senses; accustomed to distractions, they have a great deal of difficulty."

Actually, prayer begins at the moment of desire, yet it becomes more aware, and this is why it can take shape. St. Augustine simplifies things for us by saying: "If the text is prayer, pray; if it is groaning, groan; if it is thanks, be joyful; if it is a hopeful text, hope; if it expresses fear, then fear."

The things that we feel are our mirror. If we enter into conversation with God in the spirit and attitude of the text, our prayer can only be agreeable to him. The Word has come into us, and now it is normal for it to return to him under the form of prayer. Again, this made Augustine say: "When you are listening, God is talking to you; when you are praying, you are talking with God."

We must discover that we are bearing within ourselves a "heart of prayer," as Jean Lafrance expressed it.

Maurice Zundel states: "If we go every day to the depths, to the encounter with the eternal Source, if our prayer is above all a listening to the interior word, an attention paid to the small voice of God in the depths of our heart, we will bear the Light of the world; we will spread those waves of light and love which will purify the atmosphere of its impassioned debates."[23]

It is necessary, then, in the *oratio,* to discover that hidden being in the depths of our heart. That is where the true beauty dwells that will transfigure our being.

Let us recall Peter's counsel: "Let your adornment be the inner self with the lasting beauty of a gentle and quiet spirit" (1 Pet 3:4).

As a response to the *lectio,* the *oratio* knows various expressions, as we have noted. It begins by the action of grace and continues by enumerating the causes of this joy.

The *anamnesis* (the remembrance) is a sweet moment which can bring tears to our eyes. We feel transported; we want to call our friends, the faithful, all believers, in order to communicate to them this experience which nonetheless remains ineffable. To be sure, this sensation cannot be habitual and daily, but sometimes it is reserved for us, and we should then accept it with thanks and, above all, not try to contain it. Let us recall David's dance before the ark, the joyous outbursts of the prophetess Anna, of Zechariah, of Elizabeth and of Mary in the events which surrounded Jesus' birth.

It is then, in a heart thus prepared, that true Christian prayer can spring up. This prayer of entreaty, so dear to God's heart, can also be done after the manner of that of Judah to his brother Joseph, who had become the palace master of the Pharaoh of Egypt: "O my lord, let your servant please speak a word in my lord's ears..." (Gen 44:18).

Unfortunately, a pagan heritage has given us a false notion of prayer, according to which one asks God for something which one thinks can be obtained by force of words. On the contrary, authentic Christian prayer is born from the Word of God and is nourished by it. This is far from the babbling about which Matthew puts us on guard: "When you are praying, do not heap up empty phrases as the Gentiles do" (Mt 6:7).

The psalmist understood well in what dialogue with God consists of when he wrote: "Even before a word is on my tongue, O Lord, you know it completely" (Ps 139:4). The prophet, for his part, proclaimed to supplicants: "Then you shall call, and the Lord will answer" (Isa 58:9).

Finally, this prayer ends with recourse to the Trinity: "I ask for this favor in the name of the Father..." for it is toward God who is thrice holy, as the Book of Revelation tells us (cf. Rev 4:8), God who is one and three, that all prayer of thanks and petition should be addressed to be truly Christian and also liturgical: "First of all, then, I urge that supplications, prayers, intercessions and thanksgivings be made" (1 Tim 2:1).

Paul understood this well, since he ends his Letter to Timothy, where it was a matter precisely of Christians' liturgical prayer, by these words of praise to the Trinity:

"In the presence of God, who gives life to all things, and of Christ Jesus...I charge you to keep the commandment without spot or blame until the manifestation of our Lord Jesus Christ, which he will bring about at the right time...the King of kings.... It is he alone who...dwells in unapproachable light...to him be honor and eternal dominion. Amen" (1 Tim 6:13-16).

Finally, if there is a prayer that every Christian should prefer, it is the Our Father. This prayer is found within the range of the lips and of the heart, especially when the former seemed to be sealed and the latter seems like stone. It is the prayer of the Lord, which he bequeathed to us for ever and ever.

Let us recall that neither the liturgy of the East nor that of the West ever repeat the Our Father without preparation, without reminding the assembly of the marvel that this prayer is. Even today the Latin Church, to which we belong, still says, "We have the courage to say..." The liturgy of St. John Chrysostom, used in a large part of the Orthodox Church, introduces the Our Father in its own fashion. Let us join these brothers and sisters in the faith in saying:

Prayer

"Make us worthy, Lord, to dare in joy and without presumption to call upon you, O God of heaven, Father, and to say to you:

Our Father
who art in heaven, hallowed be thy name,
thy kingdom come, thy will be done
on earth as it is in heaven.
Give us this day our daily bread,
and forgive us our trespasses
as we forgive those who trespass against us;
and lead us not into temptation,
but deliver us from evil."
Amen.

Contemplatio

Contemplatio is an elevation of the soul to God where it tastes of incomparable joys, the first-fruits of eternal joys. It is the patient and sweet renunciation of our resistance. It is a faithfulness in silent waiting. The definition of contemplation takes only one phrase: being able to wait.

Here is the prayer before *contemplatio* as suggested by Guigo:

"Lord Jesus, Son of the living God, make my heart thirst for a love so great that your Spirit may give me a share in the communion of the love of the three divine persons in the silence which transcends every word and every feeling."

—Keep silence and remain still, in deep recollection.

Keeping silence means to expand, to gather oneself, to go into a state of readiness, to re-enter oneself in order to meet the one who is dwelling there: "God often pays us a visit," says Tauler, "but most times we are not at home." This phrase echoes a text, long renowned, by Augustine:[24]

"Late have I loved you, O beauty so ancient and so new! Late have I loved you! Ah, yes: you were within and I looked for you outside, where I rushed about, very mistakenly, among the beautiful things here below, your works.

"You were with me while I was not with you, kept far from you by those things which, unless they were in you, would not exist. You called and cried out to me, and you broke through my deafness. You were within me, and I was outside" *(Confessions).*

Yes, God's visits are to be taken seriously. Here is a story that sounds somewhat legendary, but which nevertheless holds a truth that only caution prevents from transmitting with all its authenticity. It has much to say about God's passage through a life.

One day, a pastor said to his sacristan:

"Have you noticed the shabbily dressed old man who goes into the church every day around noon and comes right back out? I have been watching him through a window from the rectory. This is disturbing me a bit because there are some valuable objects in the church. Try to find out what he's up to."

The next day, the sacristan waited for his visitor and approached him:

"Tell me, friend, what makes you come like this to the church?"

"I come to pray," the old man calmly said.

"Well, now! You don't stay long enough for that. You

only go up to the altar and then you leave. What's the point of that?"

"That's right," answered the poor old man. "I'm not able to make a long prayer. Still, I come every day at noon and I simply say to him, 'Jesus, I am Simon.' And I feel that he hears me."

A short time later, old Simon was run over by a wagon and was being cared for in a hospital.

"You always have such a cheerful mood despite your bad luck," a nurse said to him one day.

"That's thanks to my visitor," Simon answered her.

"Your visitor?" the nurse replied, surprised. "I haven't seen anybody here. When does he come?"

"Every day, at noon. He stands there, at the foot of my bed, and he says to me, 'Simon, I am Jesus!'"

No comment is needed on this anecdote....

Now, there comes a time when the Word ceases to bring us closer to God in order to lead us into the depths where our baptismal grace lies. St. John Chrysostom says that when anyone is baptized he is enlightened by this grace, but then it takes refuge right away in our unconscious. All the deep activity of the baptized one consists in accepting and in bringing up this baptismal grace which is in some way buried in the depths of his being, after the manner of a hidden source which feeds the jet of water in a pond.

Contemplation heals us little by little of that complex of being a sinner who imagines that God is incapable of calming his desires. To seek for satisfaction outside of God is to repeat once again Augustine's mistake:

"You were within me and I was outside. And it was there that I looked for you. My ugliness hid what was beautiful in you. You were with me, but I was not with you." How could God not fulfill the desire that he himself had implanted?

"Make room in yourself, and I will become a torrent...."

We have no more need to give thanks, to cry out, to ask. We have only to let the Word mount up to heaven like incense, peacefully, without noise. This is the phase of the ineffable groanings of the Spirit (Rom 8:26), of rest in God. We taste the prayer, the *oratio,* as Elijah tasted the cake made by the widow of Zarephath: "The jar of meal will not be emptied and the jug of oil will not fail until the day that the Lord sends rain on the earth" (1 Kings 17:13).

We will quench our thirst as did Hagar in the desert when she noticed the well (cf. Gen 21:19). We will perceive Jesus' physical presence as did John at the Last Supper.... We will have a heart-to-heart conversation, tranquil and peaceful with God and in God, without worrying about maintaining this nearness by uttering words. Silence takes the place of language.

Not a word more is said, much like old loving couples, for whom their presence and the remembrances of their common history are enough to convey love. This is what made Guigo, that master of *lectio divina*, say: "The more I know you, the more I want to know you."

In *contemplatio* we are doing an apprenticeship in a long and patient shedding which will lead us toward faithfulness. It is a matter of using time in God's company. Wait! There is the key word, we might say. That is what it is to be faithful in a Christian regimen.

In *contemplatio* we are sentinels on duty: "Post sentinels; prepare the ambushes" (Jer 51:12). We watch for the dawn to be the first, if not the only ones, to see it rise over our lives.

To be sure, dryness can make this phase of *lectio divina* laborious, even painful, since this nearness of the soul to God comes not from nature but from grace. This is why it is necessary to knock at the door of God's heart in prayer, to knock insistently like the importunate friend of the Gospel (cf. Lk 11:5ff.).

Better yet, it is necessary to listen to Christ knocking on the door of our heart until, worn out and beaten, we might give in and listen to his voice and above all open wide the door of our heart to him, of our understanding, according to the biblical expression. It is then that we will be surprised to learn that he has already gone before us....

Then, as at Emmaus, he will come in and sit at our table, and it is in the contemplation of this mystery that the bread will be broken for us and that our eyes will open. To our great astonishment, we will understand why a devouring fire burned in our hearts while Christ was breaking with us the bread of his Word (cf. Lk 24:32).

Contemplation is not a state accessible to us by our own means and even less by our own efforts. It is the ripe fruit issuing from our prayerful reading.

Contemplation is a concurrence of action: ours and Christ's. This action tends toward an ultimate accomplishment which is that of tranquil presence, of which we spoke at the beginning.

Christ acts somewhat like a catalyst which has the property of accelerating a chemical process. Here it is a matter of Christ's presence which, so to speak, clings to our being and can, on certain occasions, become palpable and visible.

If distraction comes to draw us away from this presence, we will hear Martha's voice telling us along with Mary, her sister: "The Teacher is here and is calling for you" (Jn 11:28).

Contemplatio is nothing else but this: neither ecstasy nor extraordinary revelation. It is an experience of gazing...an experience of faith and not of a vision, as the Apostle Paul advises us in his Second Letter to the Corinthians: "We walk by faith, not by sight" (2 Cor 5:7).

Mary, the mother of Jesus, is the model and mistress of contemplative prayer, because she is silence who listens. At the angel's annunciation, she listens with all her being, with her heart and her mind. When she asks a question, it is so as to understand better in order to accept more freely the mysterious design which God wants to accomplish in her. Thus she enters into communion with the Father's holy will.

Contemplation is an experience which only the interior being is called to live. This is why it is a free gift, an illumination. May the prayer which Paul addresses to the Ephesians be realized for us in contemplation:

Prayer

> "I pray that the God of our Lord Jesus Christ, the Father of glory, may give you a spirit of wisdom and revelation as you come to know him, so that, with the eyes of your heart enlightened, you may know what is the hope to which he has called you, what are the riches of his glorious inheritance among the saints, and what is the immeasurable greatness of his power for us who believe, according to the working of his great power" (Eph 1:17-19). Amen.

Actio

Actio consists of making fruitful in our lives what the Word has taught us. It comes to coordinate the soul's longings and the deeds of every day.

Guigo suggested this prayer before ending the *contemplatio:*

"Lord Jesus, Son of the living God, Word of God become man, be in me the fulfillment of the divine light and tenderness received from Sacred Scripture. You who have eaten, slept and worked, teach me to manifest only you when I eat, sleep and work, and in every other activity of my life."

It seems unnecessary to remind the disciple given over to *lectio divina* that he proceed to realize and to witness to what he has seen and heard, as the Apostle John said in his first letter: "We declare to you what was from the beginning, what we have heard, what we have seen with our eyes, what we have looked at and touched with our hands, concerning the word of life—this life was revealed, and we have seen it and testify to it...we declare to you what we have seen and heard...so that our joy may be complete" (1 Jn 1:1-4).

In other words, the baptized who hears the Word should become the actualizer of the Word and thus be assured of building upon rock: "Everyone then who hears these words of mine and acts on them will be like a wise man who built his house on rock" (Mt 7:24).

It is a matter of putting into action the Word of God and so to become a mother, brother and sister to Jesus, because we are doing the will of his Father: "For whoever does the will of my Father in heaven is my brother and sister and mother" (Mt 12:50).

We can compare the transformation which takes place in the heart of one who is assiduous in *lectio divina* to what happens in the life of one who is nourished daily by the Eucharist: this nourishment can become redemption or condemnation: "For all who eat and drink without discerning the body, eat and drink judgment against themselves" (1 Cor 11:29).

The Word is that two-edged sword which is mentioned in the message of the angel to the Church of Pergamum. We should also hear it said: "You did not deny your faith in me even in the [difficult] days" (Rev 2:13).

Still, this desire for transformation has to be humble and confident. This is what made St. Philip Neri, that figure of the Italian Renaissance, say: "Lord, the wound in your side is large, but if you do not help me, I am capable of making it still larger."

To receive the Word as Mary did is also the surest way to make it bear fruit in our life. Like her, going to visit our neighbors and bringing Jesus to them in some way can make them feel Jesus stirring within them at our approach (cf. Lk 1:44).

Thus the Word will produce what we wish to see accomplished: "For it is God who is at work in you, enabling you both to will and to work for his good pleasure" (Phil 2:13).

This is, according to Paul, to be "in the midst of a crooked and perverse generation, in which you shine like stars in the world" (Phil 2:15).

Lectio divina is thus more than a school of prayer; it is above all an experience of life.

Ambrose outlines well the transition from *lectio divina* to concrete life: "*Lectio divina* leads us to the practice of good actions. Indeed, just as meditation on words aims at memorizing them, so that we might recall the meditated words, so meditation on the law, on the Word of God, inclines us toward action, and drives us to act. Acting this way in God will aid the quality of our fraternal relations."

Teresa of Avila (1515-1582), trustworthy for her realism, uses the same language as Ambrose after the span of more than a millennium: "Do not seek to be helpful to the whole world, but to those who live in our company."

It is also a simple matter to recall, in the fire of action, the presence of God: repeat the passage retained in the *lectio*. Make it into a short prayer. In his letter to his friend Proba, St. Augustine mentions the short prayers of the monks of Egypt: "They make frequent but very brief prayers, rapid as arrows being shot, for fear that their attention, so necessary for someone praying, might wander and become dulled in overly long prayers."

Since it is living, the Word of God should pervade one's whole life and being. The author of the Letter to the Hebrews is eloquent on this point: "Indeed, the word of God is living and active, sharper than any two-edged sword, piercing until it divides soul from spirit, joints from marrow; it is able to judge the thoughts and intentions of the heart. And before him no creature is hidden, but all are naked and laid bare to the eyes of the one to whom we must render an account" (Heb 4:12-13).

Let those who have ears to understand, understand the Lord's message.

Prayer

> Lord Jesus Christ, king of kings,
> you who have power over life and death,
> you know what is secret and hidden,
> and our thoughts and feelings are not veiled from you.
> Heal my secret deeds.
> I have done evil [and good] in your presence.
> Lord, I praise you and glorify you,
> despite my unworthiness,
> because your mercy toward me knows no limit.
> You have been my help and protection.
> May the name of your grandeur be forever praised.
> To you, O our God, be the glory! Amen.

> Ephrem, deacon

7

The Bread and the Word

The real presence of Christ in the Eucharist [25]

*P*ope Paul VI, affirming faith in the Eucharistic real presence, writes: "This presence is termed real, not in an exclusive sense, as if other presences were not real, but rather for its excellence because it is substantial and because by it Christ, God and man, makes himself entirely present." [26]

It should be noted that the Pope does not comment on his affirmation for the simple reason that it is quite clear: in the Eucharist, there is nothing but the presence of Christ that can be called real.

The reality of the presence of Christ in the liturgy is considered in a different manner according to different circumstances. Thus, when one is baptized, the water remains water; after the baptismal ceremony, there is no talk about the real presence of Christ; nevertheless, he is the one who baptizes. When the Scripture is proclaimed, the book remains what it is in its materiality. After the proclamation of the Word, there is obviously no talk of a real presence of Christ according to this mode of presence which is the proclamation of the Word.

But when the Eucharist is celebrated, the bread is no longer bread, and the wine is no longer wine; they only have their appearances. It is for this reason that, once the celebration of the Eucharist is completed and for as long as the species of bread and wine last, we affirm, in faith, that the Eucharistic real presence of Christ remains and stays.

We are before a reality of presence which surpasses other modes of presence. Yet, once again, the Eucharistic presence does not exhaust the other modes of presence; these latter should be considered as being real and not just as symbolic or analogical.

The other modes of Christ's presence

> He is present in the sacrifice of the Mass, not only in the person of his minister, "the same now offering, through the ministry of priests, who formerly offered himself on the cross," but especially under the Eucharistic species. By his power he is present in the sacraments, so that when a man baptizes it is really Christ himself who baptizes. He is present in his Word, since it is he himself who speaks when the holy Scriptures are read in the Church. He is present, lastly, when the Church prays and sings, for he promised: "Where two or three are gathered in my name, there am I in the midst of them" (Mt 18:20).[27]

The vocational aspect of the Word

It is in liturgical celebrations that the Word appears in its provocative guise: it demands a hearing and a response in action. The Lord did not leave a book for men and women but rather sent them messengers, the apostles, and founded the Church which the apostles organized, moved by the Holy Spirit. This gave Gustave Martelet reason for writing: "Along with Scripture, the Eucharist is the twofold transcultural bread which the Lord, who is Spirit, procures for the Church so that she might stay in this world as the witness of a work not of this earth, and which binds her to the world with absolute bonds."[28]

This Word of the first messengers is still addressed to us today, especially at the moments when it is proclaimed and when it actualizes the mystery of salvation in the Eucharistic celebration. Yet this reality was forgotten for a certain period. Thus the four basilicas of Rome, St. Peter, St. Mary Major, St. Paul outside the Walls, and the Lateran, have no ambo (a raised platform from which the Scriptures were read). These are evident signs of a decadent mentality.

The architects of a certain period, and often those of our times, have seemed to have forgotten that, in the church, the altar and the ambo are the two centers forming but one. The destruction of magnificent pulpits counts among the blunders which have accelerated the departure of the faithful from our churches (a silent schism). When what is significant is removed from sacred places, they become insignificant and people desert them with no regrets.

In a conference given to his own community of Solesmes, Dom Gueranger expressed this idea: "The Sacred Scriptures have been given to us for light and the Holy Eucharist for nourishment; we have the Word under both forms."

Thus, when the Word of God is proclaimed in the liturgical assembly, Christ is really present, and his presence is no less real than that of the Eucharist.

> Doesn't Scripture have God himself as its author? It is the Word of God, the Verb of God, and thus it is truly a sacrament in the wider meaning of the term. This is so true that sometimes, in certain places in the past, in the Corpus Christi procession the Blessed Sacrament and the Gospel were carried side by side under the canopy.[29]

This comparison can help us better distinguish the fruits of the two types of presence:

The Scriptures help us to recognize the Christ of the Eucharist; the Eucharist gives us the Christ of the Scriptures. The Scriptures show us the face of Christ; the Eucharist allows us to contemplate with the eyes of faith. *Lectio divina* helps us to recognize the heart of Jesus; the Eucharist gives us the heart of Jesus.[30]

The two tables

In the church we notice that there is, at the center, a single altar but two tables: the table of the Word (the ambo), where the Good News of salvation is proclaimed; and the table where precisely the salvation brought by Jesus is accomplished, the table of sacrifice.

If we say that the altar is a table, it is because it is on this table that the bread and the wine are set. Still, it is not an exaggeration to speak of the table of the Word, "For the Word of God is eaten like good bread and drunk like pure water."[31]

Jesus said: "One does not live by bread alone, but by every word that comes from the mouth of God" (Mt 4:4).

The Word of God and the Eucharistic bread complete one another. Both are necessary for maintaining one's spiritual health.

At the celebration of the Eucharist, there is then the sequence of the Word and the Bread. When we hear the Word and it takes root in our hearts, we are already communing with Jesus who is living, because he is risen.

When we eat the Bread of Life which the priest consecrates, we are nourishing ourselves with the same Word: "And the Word became flesh and lived among us" (Jn 1:14).

If the aim of *lectio divina* consists in grasping the spiritual meaning of the Word, and the act of nourishing ourselves with the Body of Christ makes the Word more present to us, then at that point these two movements converge. It is a matter then of a single liturgy.

This is why St. Bernard uses words concerned with eating when he speaks of the Word:

> The famine in the land is the lack of the Word of God in the human spirit. It is not hunger for bread nor thirst for water which drives them greatly in Egypt, but rather hunger for hearing the Word of God. To have recourse to this Word is to take the food of the Sacred Scriptures. The Word of God is bread since it gives and preserves life in us.

These references clearly show us that the Word read in faith engenders life in the same way as do the Eucharistic bread and wine consumed in faith. The Spirit is acting both in the one and in the other.

Prayer

> The Bread and the Word,
> Two indispensable foods.
> Lord, feed me
> With your Body and your Word
> And I will be able to run along your paths.
> Lord, make me understand
> Your mysteries of salvation
> And I will see your glory
> On the face of the other.
> Lord, I am hungry, I am thirsty
> For the Bread and for the Word.
> Satiate my spirit and quench its thirst
> But not all at once...
> Lest, satisfied,
> my desire should slumber.

Conclusion

*I*n the course of these reflections on *lectio divina*, we have above all wanted to share with the baptized a precious legacy that belongs to them. We have taken it to heart to share an ancient heritage too long neglected. There is nothing new here. Yet every spiritual tradition contains hidden elements, the revelation of which puts certain values into the balance, the roots of which are more fragile. The return to secure and profound traditions can thus change the mode of living our relation with God and that of praying the Word.

From the start, these pages have been entrusted to the Holy Spirit.

His lights have been abundantly sought. There have obviously been trying moments, dry periods and even the temptation to drop it all. Yes, the shadows came despite the pleas. Yet because of them, the moments of clarity were all the more appreciated.

"In his light we see light," we sing in the Divine Office. Thus, anyone who goes to God in his Word can be sure of taking a shining path even if the shadows might make one's steps hesitant on some days.... This, moreover, is what grounded our certitude and gave us the courage to undertake writing this modest work.

Finally, we have intended to share a spiritual experience. This was a recent experience yet one practiced assiduously, with daily faithfulness guaranteeing its fruits. Teresa of Jesus, a woman experienced in prayer, said: "If we persist in prayer, it will lead us to the haven of light. In my view, losing the way is nothing else than ceasing to pray."

This, in sum, is the great lesson from all spiritual masters. May these lines convince you more of this.

That the Word should be better read, better meditated, better prayed, better contemplated and better lived has been the sole aim envisioned for helping all our brothers and sisters involved with us in this passionate adventure which is leading toward the kingdom.

In completing these pages, I would have to reproach myself if I neglected to thank my brothers, the Cistercian Monks of the Abbey of Our Lady of Nazareth in Rougemont (Quebec). They were my teachers and my inspirers. A retreat on *lectio divina,* preached by one of them, was the spark for me. Thanks to their love of the Word, the beauty of their Divine Office, the calm of their liturgy, and the silence of their monastery, "Jesus burned my heart at the crossroads of the Scriptures." For this precious gift, praise be given to the Father, "from whom all perfect gifts descend" (Jas 1:17).

Bibliography

Bianchi, Enzo. "Prier la Parole." *Vie monastique* 15, Abbaye de Bellefontaine, France, 1983, p. 108.

Fiores, Stefano and Tullio Goffi, eds. *Dictionnaire de la vie spirituelle.* Paris: Cerf, 1983.

Flipo Claude, "Invitation A la priere." *Vie chretienne,* supplement n. 189, Paris, 1977.

Guy, Jean-Claude, trans. *Paroles des anciens.* Paris: Seuil, 1976.

Hamman, Adalbert. *Abrege de la priere chretienne.* Montreal: Desclee-Novalis, 1987.

Liebaert, Jacques. *Les Peres de l'Eglise.* Vol. 1. *1st-4th Centuries,* "Bibliotheque d'Histoire du Christianisme," n. 22, Paris: Desclee, 1986.

Oury, Guy-Marie. *Chercher Dieu dans sa Parole* France: C.L.D., 1982.

Spanneut, Michel. *Les Peres de l'Eglise* Vol. 2. *4th-7th Centuries,* "Bibliotheque d'Histoire du Christianisme," n. 22, Paris: Desclee, 1990.

Gouillard, Jean, trans. *Petite philocalie du coeur.* Paris: Seuil, 1979.

Notes

1. Father Marc-Daniel Kirby, O.Cist.
2. Francois Varone, *Ce Dieu absent qui fait probleme,* p. 136.
3. Michel Hubaut, *Prier les parabolas,* p. 55.
4. Enzo Bianchi, *Prier la Parole,* p. 31
5. Maurice Zundel, *Esquisse d'un portrait,* p. 151.
6. Notes in the Jerusalem Bible.
7. Father Marc-Daniel Kirby, O.Cist.
8. Quoted by Bernard Bro in *La meule et la cithare,* p. 204.
9. André Chouraqui, *L'amour fort comm la mort,* p. 42.
10. Father Marc-Daniel Kirby, O.Cist.
11. Ibid.
12. Ibid.
13. Ibid.
14. Yvon Bonneau, O.C.S.O.
15. Father Marc-Daniel Kirby, O.Cist.
16. Francois Varone, *Ce Dieu absent qui fait probleme,* p. 167.
17. Father Marc-Daniel Kirby, O.Cist.
18. Bianchi, *Prier la Parole,* p. 54.
19. Father Marc-Daniel Kirby, O.Cist.
20. Philoxenus of Mabbug
21. Father Marc-Daniel Kirby, O.Cist.

22. Ibid.

23. Maurice Zundel, *Ta parole comm une source,* p. 13.

24. Father Marc-Daniel Kirby, O.Cist.

25. Sections 1 and 2 of this chapter are taken from the retreat of Father Marc-Daniel Kirby, O.Cist.

26. Paul VI, *Mysterium Fidei.*

27. *Constitution on the Sacred Liturgy,* n. 7.

28. Gustave Martelet, *Resurrection et eucharist,* p. 180.

29. Dom Guilmard, *Le Verbum incarnatum et le Verbum scriptum.*

30. Father Marc-Daniel Kirby, O.Cist.

31. Jean-Yves Garneau, *Decouvrir l'Eucharistie,* p. 83.

Pauline BOOKS & MEDIA

ALASKA
750 West 5th Ave., Anchorage, AK 99501   907-272-8183
CALIFORNIA
3908 Sepulveda Blvd., Culver City, CA 90230   310-397-8676
5945 Balboa Ave., San Diego, CA 92111   619-565-9181
46 Geary Street, San Francisco, CA 94108   415-781-5180
FLORIDA
145 S.W. 107th Ave., Miami, FL 33174   305-559-6715
HAWAII
1143 Bishop Street, Honolulu, HI 96813   808-521-2731
ILLINOIS
172 North Michigan Ave., Chicago, IL 60601   312-346-4228
LOUISIANA
4403 Veterans Memorial Blvd., Metairie, LA 70006   504-887-7631
MASSACHUSETTS
50 St. Paul's Ave., Jamaica Plain, Boston, MA 02130
  617-522-8911
Rte. 1, 885 Providence Hwy., Dedham, MA 02026   617-326-5385
MISSOURI
9804 Watson Rd., St. Louis, MO 63126   314-965-3512
NEW JERSEY
561 U.S. Route 1, Wick Plaza, Edison, NJ 08817   908-572-1200
NEW YORK
150 East 52nd Street, New York, NY 10022   212-754-1110
78 Fort Place, Staten Island, NY 10301   718-447-5071
OHIO
2105 Ontario Street (at Prospect Ave.), Cleveland, OH 44115
  610-621-9427
PENNSYLVANIA
9171-A Roosevelt Blvd., Philadelphia, PA 19114; 215-676-9494
SOUTH CAROLINA
243 King Street, Charleston, SC 29401   803-577-0175
TENNESSEE
4811 Poplar Ave., Memphis, TN 38117   901-761-2987
TEXAS
114 Main Plaza, San Antonio, TX 78205   210-224-8101
VIRGINIA
1025 King Street, Alexandria, VA 22314   703-549-3806
CANADA
3022 Dufferin Street, Toronto, Ontario, Canada M6B 3T5
  416-781-9131
1155 Yonge Street, Toronto, Ontario, Canada M4T 1W2;
  416-934-3440